Trust GOD, NOT MAN

"Surviving the Untold Truths"

TRACEY WILLIAMS

All scripture quotations marked NKJV are taken from the New King James Version®. Copyright © 1982 by Thomas Nelson. Used by permission. All rights reserved.

Trust God, not Man—Surviving the Untold Truths. Copyright © 2022 All rights reserved—Tracey Williams

No portion of this book may be reproduced or transmitted in any form or by any means, graphic, electronic, or mechanical, including photocopying, recording, taping, or by information storage retrieval system without the written permission of the publisher.

Please direct all copyright inquiries to:
Kingdom Trailblazers
c/o Author Copyrights
Post Office Box 767
Flora, MS 39071

Paperback ISBN: 978-1-7379781-6-9

Printed in the United States.

I dedicate this book to Rosie Lee Moore (mom), L.T Moore (dad), and Kimberly Moore (sister). All three of you played a huge impact in my life and I don't think I would be where I am today without you all. I love you all so much. Until we meet again.

I first want to thank God for allowing me to write my story. God gets all the Glory! I pray that this will help someone who has gone through a similar situation or is currently going through this situation.

Secondly, I want to give thanks to my family for always being there for me through thick and thin.

Lastly, I want to thank my niece, Corshonte Moore, for taking the time out to help me put this book together.

Table of Contents

◆

My Childhood 9

Pregnant & Confused 13

The Man of my Dreams 17

Love & Betrayal 29

My Journey to Victory 46

Dear Heavenly Father,

I want to thank You and give You all the honor, glory, and praise for allowing me to write this book. Jesus, I pray that this book helps to free someone in their spirit and find true forgiveness in their hearts. Let every word I write, and the meditation of my heart, be acceptable in Your sight.

Amen.

My Childhood

My childhood was a little unusual compared to kids' childhood today. My mother raised me to know God for myself by showing me how a Christian should live their life. My mom always prayed day and night, no matter what obstacles came her way. My mom sang in the church choir and was head of the mother's board. So, of course, she dragged me and my sister into every church where she was scheduled to sing.

Tracey Williams

My mother was a diabetic and had heart problems for as long as I can remember. Oftentimes, she would get sick and have to go to the hospital and stay for days. She never made excuses for anything, and she would always make the best out of every situation.

She made sure she taught my sister and me how to be ladies. She would make us clean, cook, and wash all the time while always listening to gospel music on the radio. Later down the road, in 2005, her diabetes took a turn for the worse, and my mom had to go on dialysis.

I can recall her saying that she didn't want to do the dialysis treatments and that she would rather go home to be with the Lord, and ultimately, God answered her request. She only went a few times before the Lord called her home. I will never forget one of her favorite scriptures, which was John 14:1-3 KJV, *"Let not your heart be troubled: ye believe in God, believe also in me. In my Father's house are many mansions: if it were not so, I would have told you. I go to prepare a place for you. And if I go and prepare a place for you, I will come again, and receive you unto myself; that where I am, there ye may be also."*

Growing up, my father's motto was, *"No job is too hard or too big for anyone that lives under my roof."* My father had a job at a local warehouse until the evening and worked nights at a company called Ready Mix, just to make sure that we had the bare necessities. He wasn't home much and had his own business at the house where he fixed tires. We also had a hog farm where we had plenty of pigs. In order to save money on food, my dad planted a huge garden every year.

> **NO JOB IS TOO HARD OR TOO BIG FOR ANYONE THAT LIVES UNDER MY ROOF!**

As kids, we always had work to do around the house. We thought it was so unfair because we didn't really have a childhood except on Sunday. Sundays were always considered the Lord's Day. That's when we would go over to my grandma's house where she would fix enough food to feed an army. All the kids in the neighborhood would come by my cousin's house—which was next door to my grandma's house—to play kickball.

That one day a week seemed like a holiday because we would always eat good food and have lots of fun. We enjoyed ourselves as kids. Sometimes we went over to my house, where we had a full basketball court. It was an old dirt court and lots of kids would come there to play with me and my siblings. That's where I discovered I had a gift for playing basketball.

I remember in seventh grade, when I started playing on the junior high team during school hours, the high school coach discovered me and asked me to try out for the varsity team. I agreed to try out. Not that I doubted myself, but I made the team! However, my parents didn't agree with it because that meant I would be away from home a lot. They said 'no' to me being on the team. I was so saddened by it, so my brother stepped in and convinced them to finally allow me to play.

It was an unbelievable ride that led me to a starting position on the team. I went on to become a point guard on my high school team at Madison Central. I had plenty of offers to attend big-time colleges until my senior year, when I became pregnant and didn't know what to do.

Pregnant & Confused

I begged my mom to let me get an abortion and, like I said, my mom was like God Himself, so she did not agree with that. After crying and pleading, I finally talked her into signing the papers so that I could get one, but she cried during the whole process because she did not want to help me with it.

After all of that, can you believe I became pregnant again? My mom started thinking she had done all that reacting for nothing, and that my pregnancy was a part of my punishment for doing things I wasn't supposed to be doing.

I ended up losing that child, and my mom told me she was fed up with me. At the young age of 21, my mother forced me to get married, and eventually, I got pregnant two more times.

The last child was a boy, and he lived one day. Yes, this was my turning point. I was mad at God because I felt like He just kept taking my children. I would get depressed many times and wanted to die. At that point, I was married and wanted to have children, so I began to pray. I prayed like I'd never prayed before. I know my mom had to be praying as well.

When I got pregnant the fourth time, I had to stop working and be on bed rest for the entire pregnancy. I was hooked up to a machine that monitored my contractions, and I had to take 24 pills a day—four pills every six hours—to try to keep the baby.

I felt like giving up many times, but my mom and sister wouldn't let me. They kept me encouraged and inspired me to keep going. My mom came over every day to make sure I was all right and prayed for us. She would lay her hands on my stomach and talk to the baby. My husband was on the road driving trucks, so my sister moved in with me to take care of the baby and me.

Finally, after about 33 weeks, my water broke, and I had to be rushed to the hospital. During the pregnancy, every sonogram showed my baby would be a girl, but upon delivery, it was a lovely boy. I was excited and grateful that God decided to complete my family.

> **THEY KEPT ME ENCOURAGED AND INSPIRED ME TO KEEP GOING.**

I felt like God had finally forgiven me for all the irresponsible things I had done. My marriage lasted 14 years, and we were together for 18 years. He was my high school sweetheart.

From that marriage, I gained an awesome son, and I began to walk in my calling as a barber. Never would I have thought I would be cutting hair, but during the marriage I learned I was anointed for it.

Later, I started my own business and now I own a barbershop and a barber school to help others get their license as a barber or stylist.

3

The Man of my Dreams

Fast forward to 2010 when I met my second husband.

It all started in February at a small Missionary Baptist Church. I had been a member since I was a little girl. This is the church I attended every Sunday as a child. I helped with summer feeding, aka "Whip Booty" for children, and so much more.

I saw at least three other pastors at the church before I met the person who I thought would be the love of my life. I would go to church time after time, listening to praise and worship, and taking in the message for the day.

One day, after service, the pastor shook my hand and asked, "How are you today?"

With my head down, I responded, "I'm fine, Pastor. Thanks for asking!"

I was so excited to talk to him because he was so intriguing. Weeks passed and he came again. This time, he asked me why I wouldn't look at him, and I turned and walked away.

> **I WAS SO EXCITED TO TALK TO HIM BECAUSE HE WAS SO INTRIGUING!**

From there, I started singing in his group, just so I could see him more. I went to the extreme of taking care of my pastor. I even made sure I cooked meals so that he could eat.

I decided to tell my friend about what the pastor had said to me, regarding why I wouldn't look at him. She laughed and said that he'd said that I was scared to look him in his eyes. I told her I never thought of it like that, so of course I encouraged myself that if he spoke to me again, I was going to look him directly in his eyes and ask him, "What do you see now?"

The next week, the opportunity presented itself. I was walking by, and he said, "Hey Stacy. How are you today?"

I looked up with a smile, stared directly into his eyes, and asked, "What do you see now?"

His eyes immediately enlarged, and he was so astonished at my response. He started blushing. I think he was more excited by my response than I was that I had gathered enough courage to look at him.

I turned and walked away. I got into my vehicle, called my friend, and told her what had happened. She couldn't believe I had done it. We were both shocked.

I thought it was time to test the waters, but little did I know I was a target from the start.

A few years earlier, I had invited pastor and his wife to dinner at my house, along with my boyfriend and my family. My mom always taught me to take care of my pastor by cooking for him and inviting his family over. After church one Sunday, I was standing around after service, along with a few other church members. I was talking about what I had cooked, and the pastor's wife overheard us. She asked if I was going to invite the pastor over to eat and I told her they were welcomed to come. She told him about the invite and they both came.

Once everyone was there, we began to socialize and have a great time. The wife suggested I show them the house, and I agreed to do so. We had been all over the house. Then, suddenly, the pastor said, "You didn't show us the master bedroom's bath." I felt some type of way.

So, I asked, "Would you like to see the master bedroom?" He anxiously said, "Yes, please," so I proceeded to show him and his wife the bedroom.

When we went in, the first thing he said was, "Oh, my goodness, that sure is a big bed! What do you be doing in that bed, Sister Stacy?"

I immediately told them, "Come on. I think it's time to eat." We went and sat around the table and began eating and socializing.

Everyone was laughing, eating, and enjoying their meal. Then, suddenly, a deep conversation got started between the pastor and his wife. They shared the conversation with us, so it seemed as if everyone was on his wife's side. So, I decided to give him a break. I had a pool table under the garage, so I asked him to come outside with me to play pool. We were not out there alone. All the other guys were out there as well. I was the only lady outside because I wanted to smoke a cigarette. As we stood outside, we began to talk while the others were shooting pool. I enjoyed his conversation.

> **I DECIDED TO GIVE HIM A BREAK.**

Years passed, and the pastor and his wife separated. During that time, I was single but having an affair with one of the deacons in the church. It had gotten so serious that the deacon wanted us to move in together. Eventually, I started feeling bad about what we were doing. He was married. Thank God for deliverance!

I tried telling him we shouldn't do this anymore. He got furious and said, "You will always be mine until you get the tag on your toe (meaning until death)."

After the encounter with the pastor, and after his divorce, he started texting me and I would respond. We really hit it off!

The Sunday before Valentine's Day in 2010, my son, niece, and I were at church. At the end of the service, the pastor walked over to me and asked what I was doing for Valentine's Day.

I told him that the kids and I were going to eat at Chili's. After that, I needed to go cut my brother's hair, who was currently in the hospital.

The pastor stated he likes to eat and asked if he could go with us. I gave him the okay. We arrived at the restaurant first and were seated as we waited for his arrival.

Once he made it, we began to order our food. We had the best conversation! The kids enjoyed it as well. I said to myself, I think this could go somewhere.

When the waiter brought the check, the pastor immediately said he would pay. I was impressed. Not only did he take care of the ticket, but he got me a gift as well.

As we were leaving the restaurant, he said, "Wait a minute! I have something for you!"

He went to his car and brought me the most beautiful roses a girl could ever have. I blushed from ear to ear, and could hear the kids in the back saying, "He likes her!" After I received my roses, I had to give him a hug and say thank you. Our date was officially over, but my life as the pastor's girlfriend had just begun.

> **NOT ONLY DID HE TAKE CARE OF THE TICKET, BUT HE GOT ME A GIFT AS WELL.**

As I was driving away, I couldn't stop thinking about the conversations. He was a charmer. He was funny. He was smart, and loved to eat.

So, the dating began. We really didn't want anyone to know we were together, especially the members of the church. We knew that would be disastrous.

We never talked on the phone. We always texted. I guess he was shy and so was I. We got closer and closer, and shared different things about our lives with other past relationships. We discussed our line of work, our interests, dislikes, and much more.

Let me remind you, we were dating secretly, and he was still the pastor of the church I was attending. It was kind of exciting for me. During this time, I was not saved at all! I was just a religious acting member, playing church, and I didn't really understand what it meant to give my life to Christ.

Now I know that Romans 10: 9-10 KJV says, *"That if thou shalt confess with thy mouth the Lord Jesus, and shalt believe in thine heart that God raised him from the dead, thou shalt be saved. For with the heart man believeth unto righteousness; and with the mouth confession is made unto salvation."*

At this phase in my life, I was enjoying what I thought was life. All the time, however, God was preparing me for my greater, but I had to go through the storms.

After dating for a while, I decided I didn't want to hide our relationship anymore. He was afraid he would lose the church. So, I agreed to further the charade.

He was so romantic. He would invite me over to his house, cook dinner for me, and then serenade me with his singing. And yes, he could sing. This man was an A+ in my book. He couldn't do any wrong in my eyes.

Trust God, Not Man!

As time passed, we were at the MS Reservoir, walking and holding hands, and we saw someone we knew from another church. It was close to his anniversary at the church, and he said he had a surprise for me.

He asked me if I could be his escort to walk in with him. I was shocked but pointed out that if we did that, everyone would know we were dating and he exclaimed, "I don't care!"

I eagerly agreed to walk beside the man of my dreams. This was unbelievable. I guess I was so excited about this relationship because in the past, I had other relationships that failed. They were not of God and there I was, dating a preacher, who was the best man I had ever been with in my life.

Even though I knew I was a sinner, I still had love for God. It was time for the anniversary. We had matching outfits! We were ready! I still remember the colors—gray and burgundy.

> **EVEN THOUGH I KNEW I WAS A SINNER, I STILL HAD LOVE FOR GOD.**

We looked astonishing! All eyes were on us as we entered the church. The members and the visitors stood as we walked in. I was like a little girl at the candy store. As he escorted me to my seat, I could hear the whispering, but I didn't care because I felt like royalty. I felt as if a queen was gracing her throne.

Just when I thought the day couldn't get any better, when it was his time to speak, he got on one knee and popped the big question, "Will you marry me, Stacy?"

I started to cry because I was so happy. I was overwhelmed with emotions. I felt like God had finally sent me a God-fearing man that could help me straighten my life up.

I replied, "Yes! Yes!" We hugged and I kissed him on his jaw. Suddenly, the crowd began to clap in excitement for us. Not everyone was excited, but some were.

The deacon I used to date had gotten the news about our engagement and began to start arguments with the pastor, my now fiancé. I began to pray and ask God how I should handle the situation. I really needed God to order my steps. There was no other alternative but to tell him about the affair.

We met up at his house to talk about our past because I didn't want it to mess up our future. As we sat in his office, I was so embarrassed. I felt as if he was going to think I was less of a woman and leave me.

He was thrilled to know that was why the deacon had been picking fights with him. This way, he knew a better way to handle things. I was so relieved. I was finally able to release that burden.

He said, "I got something to tell you about me." I guess this meetup turned into a "let it all out session!"

I replied, "Let's hear it!" He told me that he had a one-night stand with one of the members of the church, also.

By this time, I told him we both needed Jesus. I couldn't get mad because we were doing the same thing.

This day in time people put pastors on pedestals, as if they can't make mistakes. The Bible says in Proverbs 24:16 KJV, *"For a just man falleth seven times, and riseth up again: but the wicked shall fall into mischief."*

1 John 1:9 says, *"If we confess our sins, He is faithful and just to forgive us of our sins and to cleanse us from all unrighteousness."*

So, finally, all the secrets were out, and we could move on since we knew God, and had put all that behind us. Now, it was time to plan my wedding with the love of my life.

4

Love & Betrayal

We came up with a wedding date and married that same year. I know it happened soon! We had just gotten engaged in June. We were in love and wanted to be together forever.

People began to talk and ask, "Why are you rushing it? Why are you two so anxious to marry?" My life was in speed mode, and I couldn't stop it. All the church members, family, and friends were warning me not to get married. They were saying that I barely knew him. They would say that he had already been married twice, and I was the third wife. I didn't care anything about what they were saying. I didn't want to hear it. I was ready to marry the man of my dreams, so I thought.

I did as the Bible says, *"And above all things have fervent love for one another, for love will cover a multitude of sins."* 1 Peter 4:8 NKJV.

> **I WAS READY TO MARRY THE MAN OF MY DREAMS, SO I THOUGHT.**

My love for God had grown, and I thought that if God could forgive us for all the wrong we had done, then why couldn't I forgive him of his accusations?

I didn't listen. I still made plans to marry the man of my dreams. Their talks didn't work, so they had to come up with another plan to keep us from getting married. The church called a business meeting to talk about firing him. This was the craziest meeting ever in church history, I suppose.

Trust God, Not Man!

Everyone was there to vote him out. They said he had stolen money from the church and was dating a woman in the church. So, I guess those were grounds to fire him. It was so bad. They bashed and disrespected him as a pastor; I felt sorry for him and had to do something.

I stood up and said that the pastor was not the only person doing wrong in the church. I stated that one of the deacons and I had an affair in the past. You could have heard a pin drop. It was so quiet. Everyone was looking and waiting for me to say which deacon it was. This showed how much I loved my fiancé. I was willing to take the heat off him and put it on me.

Then, the entire congregation started arguing. Seriously, you would've thought this was a club scene. This was no church at all.

The sad part is that these issues are still going on in churches today. The main reason some people do not want to attend church is because they do not see the church any differently than the world. As Christians, we are supposed to be peculiar people, meaning we're to be set apart from the world.

After all this commotion, the pastor still didn't want to give up his position at the church. I asked him to please give it up because I felt we were never going to be at peace there. After giving it some thought, he finally agreed.

Then, it was back to wedding planning! It was very stressful because everything was extremely expensive. He didn't have any additional income. He had a job, but all his money was accounted for. Basically, I had to pay for the entire wedding. I loved this man with all my heart, and I wasn't going to let money interfere.

Time went on and we were no longer at the church. The members said that we couldn't have the wedding there because we were no longer members. I talked to my dad because he was one of the head deacons at the church around this time. I told him that the bylaws stated that if I was paying tithes there, I was supposed to be treated as any other member with the same rights and privileges. My dad talked to the deacon board, and they couldn't stop it. We were approved to have the wedding there.

It was time for the wedding. November 6, 2010, came, and was the happiest day of my life! My fiancé's daughter came in from Texas and we were excited.

Trust God, Not Man!

I cooked breakfast that morning before I left for the beauty salon, where my best friend was styling my hair. I felt exceptional because she closed her shop for me to get my hair styled.

As we sat talking about all the rumors, I told her I was still going through with it. But it was clear she wasn't on the same page. I asked why couldn't she just be happy for me? She said that she was happy for me, but she just thought that I was making a quick decision, with no thought. She also stated that she saw devil horns whenever she looked at him. I didn't know what to say. I was the only person there, and I was an hour late for my wedding.

During that time, I got several calls about how church members were still having choir practice and the decorators couldn't decorate the church. I began panicking! My hair was not styled, and the church was not ready! What else could possibly go wrong?

Now, this charming man, who would soon be my husband in about an hour, flipped the script on me. He called me and went off! He asked me where the hell I was. He stated that his family and friends were there, but I was not, and even asked if I was canceling the wedding.

I told him to calm down and explained that I was still at the beauty salon and my hair wasn't styled. He refused to believe it since I had been away from the house since 7:30 that morning. He was furious with me! That's when all I thought was good went bad.

I finally arrived at the church, got dressed, and was ready to walk down the aisle. We made it through the wedding.

I was Mrs. Stacey Wilkinson, and we were headed to the Bahamas for our honeymoon. I was excited because I had never been overseas before. I had spent a lot of money on this wedding and honeymoon. I had probably spent close to $10,000. I was thinking, I just know he's going to fund the spending for the honeymoon! I was wrong! He said he didn't have money to spend for us to have a good time. I overdrew my account so that we could enjoy our honeymoon.

> **I WAS MRS. STACEY WILKINSON.**

At that point, I started to wonder what's really going on here?

Trust God, Not Man!

The honeymoon ended, and we were back in the real world. We didn't have a church to attend, and he was no longer pastoring. He had a job with an investment company, but it didn't pay good money. At that time, I was working at a barbershop and brought home enough to take care of the bills.

He had multiple personalities. Some days, he would be so loving and kind. Sometimes I would come home, and he would have dinner ready and afterward, give me a foot massage because he knew I had been standing all day.

Other days, he was mean and selfish. He blamed me for losing the church. He would always say, "I don't have money like I used to because wanting to be with you cost me my church!"

That hurt me so badly; I would just cry. I used to ask God, *"Did I make a mistake?"*

We decided to visit a church not far from where we lived and after going twice, my husband just jumped and joined the church. He did not talk to me about it. He just got up and went down to the altar. I was so embarrassed because people were looking at me as if I was allowing my husband to join by himself, so I went down as well.

We were members of a church after two weeks of being married. He started playing the guitar for the church and singing, but he still wasn't satisfied because preaching is what he loved to do. About eight months passed, and the pastor of the church still hadn't asked him to preach. My husband wasn't too happy about it, so we left that church and started going to another church where he played the piano.

Once again, he never respected me enough to ask my opinion or anything. He would just do things. I wanted to be a submissive wife and honor my husband, so I didn't question his decisions about where we should serve God. I trusted him to lead us.

Time passed, and the pastor of the church asked him to preach one Sunday. He and his wife were going out of town, so he needed a replacement. My husband preached so well that they talked about it for months. My husband was the best preacher, in my opinion, and I was his biggest fan! He got this brilliant idea about restarting the ministry he had before he came to the church where I grew up.

Some of the members at the church that he played the piano for wanted to be a part of his ministry. That was when things started getting real to me because I was going into the role of First Lady Wilkinson, but I never had any training.

My husband was a very talented man. He played the piano, bass guitar, and preached. He also sang, wrote music, and even wrote a book. I was so excited for him and supported him in all his accomplishments. My husband is the father of five wonderful children, one stepdaughter, and one stepson.

My husband was really having a hard time in the work field at that time in our marriage. He had quit his job and became a stay-at-home husband for a while. I never belittled him, and I kept encouraging him that everything would be alright. He didn't want to feel like less of a man, so he carried his own weight around the house.

I would come home from work and dinner would be ready and the house would be spotless. He was perfect. But there were many issues that should have thrown up a red flag in my marriage that I now reflect on.

The first sign was when the deacons and trustees said that my husband had stolen money from the church. When I asked him, he denied it and said that people were jealous of him being with me, and he didn't have access to do such a thing.

Next, he allowed me to pay for the entire wedding. I was thinking that maybe he would ask some family members to help, to keep me from being stressed.

Then, he had to go to Kansas to record his CD and handle his book deal. I was so excited about going until I found out I had to fund the entire trip alone. My husband didn't care. He was a man that only wanted you to help him get to his next destination, at all costs.

He would steal, manipulate, exemplify fraudulent behaviors, and cheat to get what he wanted. When we arrived at the hotel in Kansas, he gave the lady a credit card and it declined. I was so embarrassed that I paid for it myself. Imagine how mad I was after finding out my husband was a big liar.

On top of all of that, he had a lustful spirit. His lust for women was out of this world. He was so disrespectful, and once we got to Kansas, I found out that all the women in the singing group would be riding with us everywhere we went.

I confronted him about it, and he said they didn't have money to rent a car. I told him, "Neither do you!" I went back to the hotel to cool off. He came to check on me and told me he was sorry, and he just wanted to record his CD badly.

I melted, looking into his puppy dog eyes, and told him, "Let's just get through this weekend." We completed the task at hand and returned home.

Let me remind you, my husband was very clever. That was another one of his schemes. As First Lady Wilkinson, I had no experience. We had started the church and decided to have a meeting at our home to invite the potential members. I was so excited about the ministry going forward. I cooked dinner for the evening. We had a great turnout, and I even invited my brother because I thought he would be great for the finance department of the church.

> **LET'S JUST GET THROUGH THIS WEEKEND.**

We had everything we needed, except the building. We needed money to pay the deposit and the first month's rent. I became excited again for him to start the church because I felt like it was the type of ministry where he could bring a lot of souls to Christ.

However, this was not the kind of ministry that just drew you in. If you were there, you had to want to be there. This ministry didn't cater to anyone.

The time came to look for a building. After days of searching, we finally found the perfect spot. The building had plenty of space, including stairs, a front office, and a huge warehouse in the back. The parking lot was great, also. The only flaw was it needed cosmetic work done on the inside.

We needed to have another church meeting to discuss the work that needed to be done and how to furnish the building. Everyone was excited and pitched in on the expenses because it was our ministry. I offered to let my husband use my Home Depot card with the agreement that he would help pay it off. I also gave him about $2,000 in cash to help where needed.

Even after he left me to pay for the wedding alone, our honeymoon, and the Kansas trip, I still trusted him to do the right thing. I was thinking, no man can do his wife this way and claim that he loves her, right? At that point, we were about to move into the building. Then, he announced he was going to start his own investment company. Wow! I was so excited for him to start working. I didn't think about where the money would come from to fund the business; I was just happy for him.

This was another red flag I missed. I know you are probably thinking, this woman is so naïve. What was she thinking? Love had me so blind, and I just knew I had a God-fearing husband. I trusted him. The Bible says in Colossians 2:8 NKJV, *"Beware lest anyone cheat you through philosophy and empty deceit, according to the tradition of men, according to the basic principles of the world, and not according to Christ."*

We had everything we needed to get ready to have our first service before Christmas of 2010. We had about 10 members, but we had an awesome time. The spirit of the Lord was in that place and in us. The Word was getting out about the church, and God continued to add souls to the ministry. I was excited to see different people coming. We were missing so many people in different positions. I took on the role of being the Sunday School Superintendent. Eventually, we got a Sunday School teacher.

Everything was going well, or so I thought. The entire time, the Sunday School teacher was after my husband. He was leading her on and telling different people in the church that he needed a more spiritual woman. So, now, on top of the other red flags, I felt useless and unworthy of being First Lady.

My husband always belittled me, not only at church, but at home as well. He never wanted me to talk to the ladies of the church. He would express to me how he didn't want me to run his ministry. The entire time, he was infatuated with all the women at the church. Even still, I loved my husband so much that I would put on programs and raffles to earn money to help support the church.

Later, the church started to crumble. Members started arguing with each other. Within the building, my husband started his investment company. I was suspicious and curious as to where he got the money for everything. About nine months later, I got a slap in the face from a credit card company seeking a debt from me for over $30,000.

I told the creditor I had never applied for a credit card. They asked me personal questions that only a person of interest would know. I decided to ask my husband if he had stolen my identity. He lied at first and then after several weeks, when I finally decided to let it go, he decided to tell the truth and confessed to doing it. He said that he would pay the bill on his own.

Trust God, Not Man!

I was devastated! The man that I trusted and cared for manipulated and stole from me. I didn't know what to do. I could not tell anyone because I didn't want to lose my husband and ruin his ministry. All I could do was call on the name of Jesus. He kept me from becoming an angry, bitter, and scorned First Lady.

Yes, I stayed with my husband. The vows said, "for better or worse." I didn't believe in divorce, so if this marriage wasn't going to work, it was not because I abandoned the marriage. After being at that location for about two years, my husband started looking for another building because we couldn't afford that one anymore. He didn't tell the members. He told them that "God was taking us up higher to a better location."

Mind you, I was a submissive wife and wouldn't dare go against my husband. I was establishing a closer relationship with God and my desire was and still is to please God in my everyday walk in this Christian race. I continued to bless the Lord through it all. One of my many gifts was to

> **GOD WAS TAKING US UP HIGHER TO A BETTER LOCATION.**

invite people to the church. The Bible calls us to be "fishermen."

We moved to a different location—an enormous church with about thirty members. We had some good service.

By that time, we had about three evangelists and women ministers attending the church. Yes, a mess it was. They all were jealous of each other. One of the evangelists left. My husband would tell me he didn't like evangelists. He liked one so much that he let her be over the women's ministry and teach Sunday School, and she never paid any tithes.

There it goes again. Another red flag! My husband also let this evangelist sit in the pulpit with him. She acted as if she was his wife and not me. Things started to get heated between us and he decided to leave me. I really couldn't understand why he did that.

The Spirit of the Lord revealed to me he had a lustful spirit for women. He also had a problem with wanting to be more than what he was. He bought an old BMW to impress women and blew through all the $30,000 that he had stolen my identity to get.

Trust God, Not Man!

I began my own investigation. I found out that he had stolen my identity for a second time and got a loan for his small finance company to buy the car. I couldn't believe it! He had done this to me again. I went and pressed charges and hired an attorney because I had two things on my credit that were not my doing.

This was like something you would see on television. Nothing hurt me more than being told there was nothing I could do about him stealing my identity, because he was my husband, so that made us one. Because of the lack of trust, resentment, and distance that had occurred throughout the marriage, I found myself no longer in love. Finally, he told me he was leaving, and I didn't put up a fight because in my heart I knew it was over.

My Journey to Victory

This is when my new journey began. I was classified as broke, busted, and disgusted. I was on my own, but with the help of my Lord and Savior Jesus Christ, He gave me strength that I never thought I would have and peace that surpasses all understanding.

The Holy Spirit was my comforter through this storm. People of God, you don't have to stay in the storm; you can come out better and stronger than ever. Luke 11:21 NKJV says, *"When a strong man, fully armed, guards his own palace, his goods are in peace."* The enemy comes to steal, kill, and destroy us. You have a choice to stay down or get up fighting for your life.

> **THE SPIRIT OF THE LORD SPOKE TO ME LOUDLY AND CLEARLY TO STAY CALM.**

Just when I thought that nothing else could possibly hurt me and things couldn't get any worse, after he left our home, two weeks later, I caught him red-handed with his soon-to-be fiancée.

At that time, I was at my place of business, a couple of blocks away. That morning, the Spirit of the Lord spoke to me loudly and clearly to stay calm. I thought to myself, "Lord Jesus, what's about to happen?" A friend came to my business, and I asked her, "Sister, can you please pray with me? Not inside my business, but inside my truck, please."

I know you're wondering, why the truck? Well, I didn't want to disturb my customers. She agreed. Before we could start praying, God told me to look up, and it was like my husband and his new woman were two feet away. My friend got scared over what I may do because I asked her to get out of my vehicle. She said, "Sister, let's pray. Get out and let's go back inside."

I agreed. As soon as she opened the door and got out, I sped off and headed straight towards the vehicle my husband and his girlfriend were sitting and chatting in. They were so into the conversation that they didn't see me pull up. But God kept me calm. I got out of my vehicle and spoke to her and told her to smile for the camera. She immediately covered her face with shame.

I addressed him and told him the same. I asked him, *"Is this how you do it now, in daylight?"* He was so inconsiderate about how I was feeling and even had a smirk on his face. If I wasn't truly saved, I would have taken his life and thought nothing of it.

God's Word says in 1 Corinthians 10:13 NKJV, *"No temptation has overtaken you except such as is common to man; but God is faithful, who will not allow you to be tempted beyond what you are able, but with the temptation will also make the way of escape, that you may be able to bear it."*

I know this may sound insane, but I still loved my husband and knew that God could restore anything He wanted to reconcile. He had only been gone for two weeks. Love doesn't leave that soon. But I realized that was me not wanting to let go of something that I did myself. I can admit it now, after five years, that I married my husband for sex. Don't judge me. I know it's selfish and misleading.

I wanted to live a righteous life before the Lord. I felt like I had everything under control except for the lust I had. So, you're saying I got what I deserved, right? Throughout the marriage, I constantly repented, asking God to forgive me. I really wanted to love my husband wholeheartedly. God can do anything above all you can ask or think. He gave me a desire to really love my husband unconditionally, no matter what he had done to me. It was past tense.

Throughout my life, I have learned so much about relationships, money, and, most of all, God.

A relationship is the state of being connected to someone by blood or marriage. When you are connected to your spouse, you become one. I've learned that in relationships, you must put God first and then your partner. If you learn to put your spouse's needs before your own, then the relationship will not be selfish. If you and your spouse are always honest and truthful with each other, it keeps away confusion.

Every relationship needs that agape love. Yes, the same love that Jesus Christ has for you and I. Learn to talk about certain issues and not hold things inside. If you hold it in, this will only cause an explosion in the end. You should never look to getting a divorce while you are married. No one could have told me I would have not one but two divorces. I began to ask God, "Why me, Lord? Is there another person who wants this job?" God knew I would learn from this and help someone else with the wisdom that He instilled in me about relationships, which is exactly why I am writing this book.

The truth is, no relationship comes with a lifetime guarantee. God allows us to go through different storms in our lives so that we can get to the things that He has in store for us. Jeremiah 29:11 NJKV says, *"For I know the thoughts that I think toward you, says the Lord, thoughts of peace and not of evil, to give you a future and a hope."*

WHY ME LORD?

I have learned to give God thanks and glory in everything. In order to move forward in your life, you must do four things: forgive, release, bless those who curse you, and pray for those who have mistreated you. God will bless you beyond what you can think of or ask for.

Trust God, Not Man!

The last thing I learned about relationships is to never let sex be the foundation of it. Once the lustful desire is gone, you won't know what to do. You won't be able to talk to each other because the conversation originated in lust; in the bed. If you aren't careful, it will cause you to seek a new victim to fulfill that lustful desire. This will keep happening until you ask God to deliver you and set you free.

Now that I've aired out all my dirty laundry, I am ready for the rehabilitation of my new life. Let's talk about what I've learned about money. The Bible says in 1 Timothy 6:10 NKJV, "*For the love of money is the root of all kinds of evil, for which some have strayed from the faith in their greediness, and pierced themselves through with many sorrows.*"

In the beginning of my book, I talked about money a lot because at the start of my marriage, I had a lot of money, but by the end of my marriage, I had lost so much. At that time in my life, I didn't know I loved money until all the arguments in my marriages were about money.

Money is not meant to control our lives. It is meant to help with our financial needs. Even though I loved money, I always paid my tithes. I guess that's why I didn't go completely broke. I did have to pay all the debt back on my own that my husband had incurred.

Malachi 3:8-10 NKJV kept me trusting in God's Word. It says, *"Will a man rob God? Yet you have robbed Me! But you say, 'In what way have we robbed You?' In tithes and offerings. You are cursed with a curse, For you have robbed Me, Even this whole nation. Bring all the tithes into the storehouse, That there may be food in My house, And try Me now in this," Says the Lord of hosts, "If I will not open for you the windows of heaven And pour out for you such blessing That there will not be room enough to receive it."*

God gave me double for my troubles! He didn't allow me to lose anything. In fact, I was blessed with more money than I ever had. All my bills were paid on time, and I was able to splurge a little. Statistics show that finances are one of the top reasons for divorce. God says when two are joined together, they become one. You couldn't tell me that back then. I felt like I worked for my money and every earning was mine.

I know you must think I'm crazy after all I've gone through with my identity being stolen and the money situations, but God is faithful. Guess what? It's just money. You can't take it with you when you leave earth, so why not bless others with it?

Trust God, Not Man!

No, I'm not saying it's okay for people to use you or take from you, but I need you to put others' needs before yours. Luke 12:48 NKJV says, *"But he who did not know, yet committed things deserving of stripes, shall be beaten with few. For everyone to whom much is given, from him much will be required; and to whom much has been committed, of him they will ask the more."*

Don't think God gave you money to stack up and hide. He wants us to help others who are in need, and not just with money, but with clothes, food, prayer, and love. There was one day at my place of business when something hit me, and I realized I've been guilty of loving money.

I had a new cell phone, and I couldn't get my Square register to work so that I could take payments. I literally lost my mind and had an attitude with everybody. My mind was on the fact that I needed to be able to get money in various ways. God immediately grabbed my attention! I repented right away! He changed my thoughts about money, and it has never been the same since that day.

Do I like what money can do? Yes, of course I do. My daily prayer is that the Lord will let me be a blessing to someone every day! An old saying of mine was, "Make the money, don't let the money make you," but that mindset no longer exists.

Last but not least, God is the author and the finisher of my faith.

I kept the faith that God would see me through all of this, and He did.

Five years after the divorce, I can truly say God has strengthened me and my heart stays on pleasing Him. My ex-husband and his wife have come to face me. I guess they wanted to see if I have truly forgiven them. I've talked and prayed with her. Yes, the same lady that was cheating with my husband. He has come to my place of business for several haircuts to see how I would react. I will admit, it was kind of awkward at first, but when I thought about how God has blessed me, he was like any other customer. I would tell him "Thank you" at the end of each service and tell him to have a good day.

Luke 17:3-4 NKJV says, *"Take heed to yourselves: If thy brother trespass against thee, rebuke him; and if he repent, forgive him. And if he trespass against thee seven times in a day, and seven times in a day turn again to thee, saying, I repent; thou shalt forgive him."*

Trust God, Not Man!

It was a journey getting to where God wanted me to be in Him, but there's no other place I'd rather be. Forgiveness is not for the other person; it is for you! You must be set free to be who God has called you to be. I'm flattered to say I answered my calling as an evangelist and will continue to spread the love of God until He calls me home to glory to be with Him.

I pray that this book helped you to understand that life can take you on a rollercoaster, but be steadfast, unmovable, and always abide in the things of God and He'll keep you in perfect peace. Amen.

Dear Heavenly Father,

This is the end of this testimony, but I know You have plenty of testimonies in me.

Thank You for the opportunity to write a portion of my life to share with the world. Thanks for allowing me to take the chains off so I can dance into my victorious season.

I pray that there is not one heart that is broken or one mind that is confused about allowing You to carry the burden of everything that consumes them. I pray that this book brings them closer to You. In Jesus's name.

Amen

"Trust God, not Man"

Why are we so quick to give our hearts away?
Seem like we give it away the very first day.

We never take the time that we need,
That's why we miss the signs to take heed.

Let us learn how to trust God
Yes, I know that sometimes it seems hard.

Jesus tells us to guard our hearts and keep our mind stayed on Him,
And He'll keep us in perfect peace and not focus on them.

This was truly a valuable lesson learned
And I wrote this book because I'm concerned.

Please!!! Help yourself while you can,
Better yet, TRUST God…and NOT man!

My Personal Prayers

My Personal Prayers

My Personal Prayers

My Personal Prayers

My Personal Prayers

About the Author

Hello, my Name is Tracey M. Williams, born in the small town of Flora, Mississippi on November 7, 1975. My parents are L.T. Moore (deceased, 2019) and Rosie Lee Moore (deceased, 2005).

I graduated from Madison Central High School in May 1994. I'm also an ordained Evangelist in the ministry (since October 2016) under the leadership of Pastor Charlie and Lady Joyce Clark at We Care Church.

I have one son, Shelby Jones, whom I'm so proud of. He has really kept me encouraged throughout my journey as a mom, as well as being an owner of several businesses: Tracey's Kuts (Est. 2013) and Executive Barber School (Est. 2018).

I was encouraged to write this book because there are so many women and First Ladies that go through so much, but they keep silent to try to protect the flock of the church. I pray that this book inspires the women who are going through a similar situation.

www.traceywilliams.org

www.ingramcontent.com/pod-product-compliance
Lightning Source LLC
Chambersburg PA
CBHW011959090526
44590CB00023B/3786